How Teddy Bears Are Made

This book is dedicated to teddy bear lovers everywhere.

With grateful acknowledgment to the staff
of the Vermont Teddy Bear Co.™ in Shelburne, Vermont,
especially to John Sortino, Fred Marks, and Spencer Putnam,
who have provided pleasure and delight for so many
children and grown-ups!

How Teddy Bears Are Made

A Visit to the Vermont Teddy Bear Factory

by Ann Morris

Photographs by Ken Heyman

Cartwheel
·B·O·O·K·S·®

SCHOLASTIC INC.

New York London Toronto Auckland Sydney

Library of Congress Cataloging-in-Publication Data

Morris, Ann, 1930 –
How teddy bears are made / by Ann Morris ; photographs by Ken Heyman.
p.   cm.
"Cartwheel books."
ISBN 0-590-47152-X

1. Teddy bears––Juvenile literature.   [1. Teddy bears.]
I. Heyman, Ken, ill. II. Title.
TS2301.T7M72 1992
688.7'24––dc20   93-44617
                                                                    CIP
                                                                    AC

12 11 10 9 8 7 6 5 4 3 2 1   4 5 6 7 8 9/9

Printed in Malaysia

First Scholastic printing, October 1994

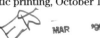

MAR   '95

Hannah has a bear.   Mbizo has a bear.   Nick has a bear.

Do you know where teddy bears come from?

Teddy bears are made in teddy bear factories, and here is a very special one. This is what you see when you come in the front door — a giant teddy bear!

Today Hannah, Mbizo, and Nick are taking a tour of the factory to find out how teddy bears are made.

They learn that the first thing you have to do when you're making a bear is to think about what it will look like.

Kathleen, the designer, thinks about bears all the time. When she's thought of a new kind of bear, she makes a drawing of it. If everyone likes the design, she makes a pattern.

Nancy lays a metal die, which is like a cookie cutter, on the fabric. A big machine stamps out many parts of the bear at one time.

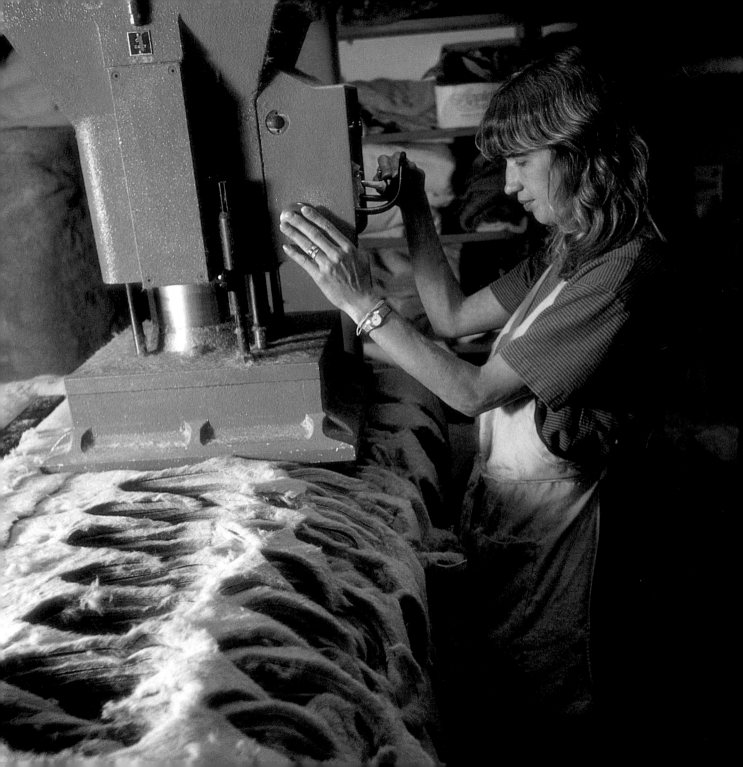

Then the ears and arms and legs
are sewn by machine.

A hole is left at the neck, so this machine can blow stuffing into the teddy bear's head. The arms and legs are stuffed the same way.

The stuffing for the body is put
in by hand, and the back of the
bear is sewn up.

Before the bears are dressed, they must
be brushed well.

Hannah, Mbizo, and Nick help brush, too.

All kinds of teddy bears are made
in this factory — artist bears . . .

ballerina bears . . .

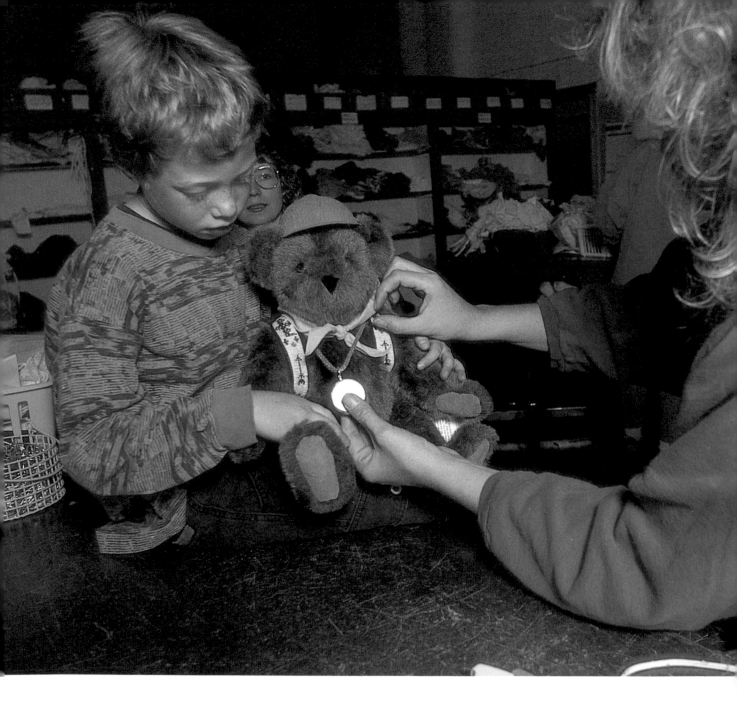

camper bears . . .

dressed-up bears, and just plain
soft, cuddly bears!

The bears get all their last-minute trimming here.

After the bears have been brushed and dressed, the people in the shipping department put tags on the bears.

This bear is ready to travel to its new home.

Telephone operators take orders for all kinds
of bears from people across the country.

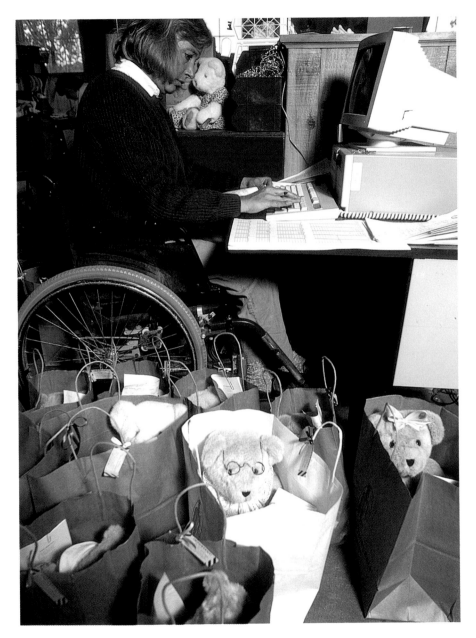

Mary Jane enters the orders
into her computer.

Then each bear is packed carefully
and mailed in a big box.

Whenever bears are torn or hurt, Dr. Sherry in the Teddy Bear Hospital knows how to patch them up. Hannah, Mbizo, and Nick watch her take care of a sick bear.

After a busy morning in the factory, Mbizo, Hannah, and Nick take their bears to lunch.

What do you think teddy bears like best to eat?